Armageddon by Casino

By

David K. Ewen, M.Ed.

ISBN-13:   978-1500398316
ISBN-10:   1500398314

<u>About The Author</u>

David K. Ewen, M.Ed. is a professor, author, speaker, talk show host, film producer, and publisher. He is the founder of Ewen Prime Company and has been in media production since 1994. In 2004, he founded Forest Academy and has toured the seven states of New York and New England on entrepreneurial studies. David is a consulting professor at the Saylor Academy in Washington, D.C. and linguistics professor in Tokyo, Japan.

David K. Ewen, M.Ed.

Project Furious 2014

"Share if you care"

About The Book

This book is me standing out front to make a statement that protects the city I live in.   It's as simple as that.   I could have chosen to sit on the side and watch the world change in front of me.   But instead, I decided to help change my community.

They say action speak louder than words.   My book, "Armageddon by Casino", and my awareness campaign effort, "Project Furious 2014", are both my actions that speak the truth about the damaging effects of casinos and why we should repeal the 2011 Expanded Gaming Act on the ballet vote on November 4, 2014.   It's as simple as that.

In some ways I have supporters.   In other ways I'm alone.   Either way, my actions are a bold move to save people and their communities.   That's not such a bad thing to do.   I'm sure those who disagree with Project Furious 2014 would agree that saving people and their communities is the right thing to do. Now we just have to educate the community on the right way to do it.

This book contains my words of understanding based on cited news reports. It takes a complicated controversial subject and puts sense to the understanding of the damaging effects casinos can have on our communities.

Because Western, Massachusetts is the first to issue a gaming license and it is close to Connecticut's casinos, I refer mostly to the impact of Casinos to this region. The information and concepts presented apply to anywhere in the United States.

To understand the geographical nature of what is described in this book, look up Springfield, Massachusetts on a map and a little over 70 miles south where two Connecticut casinos reside 11 miles apart.

Project Furious 2014

With the understanding that actions speak louder than words, PROJECT FURIOUS 2014 has adopted the slogan "Share if You Care"

ProjectFurious2014.BlogSpot.com

www.Facebook.com/ProjectFurious2014

Preface

Not in my wildest dreams would I consider taking on a controversial subject publicly.   Although, I've been in front of the public including a national audience, television, radio, and newspapers over the years, I have never been immersed in a sensitive controversial political topic.   After this one, I may continue to go back to staying out of controversy and politics.   This is different.   Throughout my life, every significant accomplishment as a child, youth, young adult, man, pet owner, church leader, and husband has been accomplished in Massachusetts.

News reports show the results of casinos moving into small communities.   This book shares them.   The effects of casino gambling and addiction to the entertainment has no possible way of being good to the community.

The facts in this book are accurate and based on cited news reports.   Might you see a typo or two in spelling? Perhaps, but that is the cost of moving fast on a significant awareness campaign such as this. Be mindful of the effort to put this together in the short time for the campaign.

A Personal Issue

The wellbeing of Massachusetts is personal to me.

- My parents were born, grew up, and live in Massachusetts
- I was born in Boston and grew up in the Boston area
- Learned to bike ride, swim, and play ball in the Boston
- Went public school in the Boston area
- Won high school running competitions in Massachusetts
- Went to college in Western, Massachusetts
- My very first care was bought in Massachusetts
- My very first apartment was in the Boston area
- Graduated with a Masters in the Boston area
- Launched my business in the metro west area in 1994
- My first radio show was in Central Mass. in 1998.

- Raised two kittens into beautiful cats in Massachusetts
- Proposed to my wife in Western, Massachusetts
- Married in Western, Massachusetts.
- Worked at companies and with clients all over the state
- Currently live house in Massachusetts
- Never lived or went to school outside of Massachusetts

From Boston Harbor to the Berkshires, every act I've accomplished has happened in Massachusetts. I am taking a stand to protect my state.

Perspective

As I currently live in Western, Massachusetts, this book looks at a perspective from Western, Massachusetts point of view.

It is a short book so read it as if it were a long article. Use it as a foundation to form your own educated opinion.   Learn what to research on your own. Use current news resources to understand what is happening in the surrounding community.

Learn more beyond this book by doing your own search on news using Google:

http://news.google.com   (News Google Search Engine)

To write this book, I spent time looking at the facts by looking at the reported news. Let this book serve as a stepping stone to your own research and education.

Support by the Public

I've been told by many people that they support Project Furious 2014. As a business owner since 1994 and founder of a nonprofit trade association in the late 1990's, I've come to find there are three kinds of supporters for a cause.

- Proactive
- Intrigued
- Cloaked

The proactive supporters are the ones who ask what they can do to help and follow through. They have it in their hearts to do whatever it takes to be supported. They never ever come up with an "I'm too busy" or "I can't make it" or "sorry, there's something else" I must do type of reason. They put priority on the effort and priority on their participation on the effort.

The intrigued supporters verbally express support, but take no action. It's like cheering on a football team, blame the coach for errors, and do it all from the couch in the living room. Their words are different from their actions. If actions dictate what is in someone's heart, then if the words are different, then the words aren't genuine to their heart.

The cloaked supporters like the idea, but won't tell anyone, even you, of they agree. They watch from the sidelines and will either hope for the underdog or the incumbent. Sometimes their opinion changes due to the outcome so that they feel justified in thinking correctly. We'll never know because they are cloaked. Either way, we don't see them.

I'm not saying "poo poo" on the intrigued or cloaked supporters. As a founder and executive of the New England Publishers Association in 1998, I am aware of the three kind of supporters one can expect from a non-profit venture. It is natural. It is what is taught at the college level. I've been a college professor since 2004 and I teach it. It is business and it is knowing people.

So Project Furious 2014 has supporters of which one of the three groups will have any actionable effect toward the success.

I'm reminded of the Italian economist who discovered in the 1860s what we call the 80/20 rule in business. 80% of your business comes from 20% of your customer base. How does this relate to Project Furious 2014? 80% of the effectiveness will come from 20% of the supporters. So between the three support groups and the 80/20 rule, Project Furious 2014, or any other cause for that matter, is truly given actionable effective support by one-out-of-five or one-out-of three supporters. The number is small, but that what is makes a good effort a challenge.

I've been running a business since 1994 and already knew the numbers by the time Project Furious 2014 launched. I accept the small number of supporters. I accept that those who do come on board have also accepted the small showing.

Finances to Run Project Furious 2014

When designing a campaign to fight a cause the associated budget leaders for the program get together to figure out how to raise funds.   Usually there is a "Donate Here" or a "Pay Here" button on website.

Instead of raising funds, I am raising awareness.   If people care about sharing the dangers of casino gaming within our communities, it doesn't cost anything for them to tell someone.   So that is what I am doing.   The effort is "on the house".   It's on me.   I'll pay for it.   I'm looking to raise awareness.   I am not raising funds.

Proponents of casino gambling will work to raises funds. I am spreading education, knowledge, and trust.   I don't need money to do that.

Already, before this book went to print, there is a blog, Facebook page, and online radio shows.   It doesn't end there.   Before this book went to print, a book release party had been scheduled for Thursday, August 7th, 2014 at 7PM at Red Rose Pizzeria on Main Street in downtown Springfield, Massachusetts.

Premise and Introduction

This book was put together based on actual news articles that talked about the effect of casinos in our community. The articles are real fact from around the country. As with anything else, our future behavior is most effective when we understand our history. Sometimes we forget history and repeat the same mistakes. We seem to have forgotten that by 1910 casino gaming was outlawed in the United States and reflected in most state constitutions. The banishment for casino gaming was for a reason. Think of the quieter more peaceful time 1910 must have been and the foundation for the decision to outlaw casino gaming. Is the year 1910 too far into the past that we have forgotten the logic behind the decision? Decades have passed and we have forgotten what casino gaming did to our society from the American Civil War to 1910.

As you read this book, remember facts and numbers don't lie. At Project Furious 2014, my opinion is obvious, but this book is not about opinions. It is based on reported facts in the news. Hopefully today's news will remind us of the decisions made in 1910.   Our past has a lot of importance.   The Constitution of the United States written and signed by young colonists guides us toward what is legally right and legally wrong.   For people of faith, the bible guides us toward what is morally right and morally wrong.

My hope is that people will be educated to the extent that they will vote no and repeal the 2011 Expanded Gaming Act and make casino gaming unlawful in the commonwealth of Massachusetts.

The supporters of casinos have the belief that revenue will be generated.   Those supporters should read this book that show news reports of casinos closing and the steady decline of casino revenue.   More competing casinos does not increase revenue.

As a country, we are just emerging from the Great Recession and still struggle with high unemployment numbers.   How does a gambling enterprise such as a casino help build communities in the long term?   What do they do for schools and our children's future? How does it help with a prosperous retirement for the elderly? In what way does it improve the health care within our community? How does a casino help the prosperity of a local business?

Sure new construction brings in jobs. What happens when the construction is done? What happens then? What about those construction jobs? Where do those people go? What is left behind? A casino. What will casino gaming and gambling going to do for our children in the long term? What benefit will an increased population of addicted gamblers do for my community? How will the theft crime caused by addicted gamblers be of any benefit? It hasn't been for the Connecticut that experienced triple theft rates since the arrival of Foxwoods and Mohegan Suns.

With an abundance of jobs in a high unemployment region like Western Massachusetts, what makes me think that the jobs will be of good pay?   And as with any business that experiences layoffs, what makes me think someone with unemployment insurance won't struggle receiving nearly half of a low paying job.   As in Connecticut that has laid off hundreds at a single time, what makes me think that won't have an impact on a small city like Springfield, Massachusetts?

The Vote

On June 24, 2014, it was announced that on November 4, 2014, Massachusetts citizens will have the opportunity to vote and repeal the 2011 Expanded Gaming Act which is the legalization of casino gaming in the state. Before that happens, it is important to know the truth behind the truth about the damaging effects of Casino gaming in Massachusetts.

The Massachusetts state Supreme Judicial Court ruled 7-0 that casino gambling should be on the fall ballot for voters to decide. This was sought by casino opponents. The concerns raised and recognized by the court include the risk of local businesses being hurt, casino promises not fulfilled, increased gambling addictions, and other related ills. In Springfield, Massachusetts, Mayor Domenic J. Sarno supports the casino plan and will not be supportive of opponents like Operation Furious 2014. MGM has been granted the first Massachusetts state license in Springfield, pending the statewide November 4th ballot vote.

Overall Effect of Casinos

PBS (Public Broadcast System) WGBH in Boston had reported on the financial aspects of casino gambling. The segment was based on the *"The National Impact of Casino Gambling Proliferation: Hearing Before the House Committee on Small Business, 103rd. Congress, 2nd. Session 77 (1994)*. There is also a lot that can be added to another report by Professor John Warren Kindt, of the University of Illinois at Urbana-Champaign who wrote "The Business-Economic Impacts of Licensed Casino Gambling in West Virginia: Short-Term Gain but Long-Term Pain".

Following the American Civil War up through 1910, there was legalized gambling in the United States. By 1910 there was essentially no legal gambling in the United States. The restriction of legal gambling was put in most state constitutions. It has been determined by 1910 that legalized gambling eventually causes the following:

1. Increased taxes
2. Loss of jobs in region

3. Economic disruption of businesses
4. Increased Crime
5. Social Welfare costs.

This is what is feared in Massachusetts and currently exists locally in Connecticut around Foxwoods and Mohegan Sun.

In our recent economic history, the activities of legal gambling has been subsidized by in one form or another by the tax payer. The costs are found in the following:

(1) Infrastructure costs,
(2) Relatively high regulatory costs,
(3) Expenses to the criminal justice system,
(4) Large social-welfare costs

AFFECT OF CRIME from CASINO GAMING

On February 26, 2012, The Associated Press reported on crime rates around Connecticut casinos since openings. In 1992, Foxwoods opened and in 1996 Mohegan Sun opened.   In 2011 Mohegan Sun generated $719 million in slot machine revenue and Foxwoods generated $650 million in slot machine revenue.   Prior to the opening, Governor Lowell Weicker warned in 1991 that the opening of Foxwoods in 1992 would lead to crime, prostitution, drunk driving, and other related crime. After Foxwoods, the first casino opened, thefts rose substantially with larcenies accounting for most of the crimes.   Today, Larceny is the largest theft crime among both casinos.   Embezzlements have more than tripled due most likely to gambling debts.   Connecticut averages about 158 embezzlement annually.   Before the casinos, the number of reported embezzlements cases averaged around 49.

In 2006, the professors, Earl Grinols at Baylor University in Texas and David Mustard at the University of Georgia completed a study on crime resulting from casinos.

They were not paid additional for this study. This was part of a faculty study at the University of Georgia. They found that except for murder, there was a rise in all crimes with 8% property crimes and 12% violent crimes when a casino was put in place. They wrote in 2006, "Specifically, problem and pathological gamblers commit crimes as they deplete their resources, nonresidents who visit casinos may both commit and be victims of crime, and casino-induced changes in the population start small but grow,".

It makes sense that murder count would not rise as significantly as theft with the arrival of a casino in the area. Residential environments and outside employment opportunities are squeezed out of casino neighborhoods. Although the murder rate as reflected as a percentage of current population can rise. It is important to understand the difference between the murder rate and murder count. The report from the Associated Press did not make that distinction.

The demographics of a casino landscape is different before the casino arrived verses after the arrival of the casino.   The choice to live near a casino is affected by traffic patterns and congestion, police reports associated with theft which reflects on neighborhood safety, and job opportunities outside of the casino.   Many businesses surrounding a casino are impacted.

With an assumed reduction of population surrounding casinos as seen near Foxwoods and Mohegan Sun in Connecticut, the count of crime may appear to be unchanged, however the rate as measured as a percentage of population may go up.   The count and rate for theft is confirmed to have gone up significantly. Therefore the overall crime rate obviously has gone up.

Declining Casino Revenue in A Growing Overcrowded Market

Evaluating a casino's financial health requires a look at the accounting books.   There is really very little that is accessible to the general public, however there are a few numbers that does get out and reach the newspapers.

The Hartford Courant newspaper in Connecticut reported in June 2014 (June 16, 2014) that Mohegan Sun reported a loss of revenue from slot machines and it supports what has been an ongoing downward trend. The revenue was reported down 5.8% from a year before.   A day later (June 17, 2014 Foxwoods reported that the slot revenues was down 9.3% from a year before.   Foxwoods also reported that the total amount wagered (called the handle) was down 2.9%.

On April 15, 2014, the Hartford Current reported in a significant decline in revenue from the total amount wagered.   The total amount wagered is also called the handle.   Foxwoods handle was down 5% from the year before and Mohegan Sun's handle was down 11% from the year before.

In July 2013, Detroit Michigan filed for chapter 9 bankruptcy due to $18.5 billion in obligations that were unfunded. Did the MGM casino in Detroit help? With our without a casino, the financial balance of a city is dependent on the economic infrastructure. A casino does not financially save cities.

The Fiscal Times reported on June 8, 2014 that casino revenue has declined in Detroit. To give comparison of casino revenue decline, the same Fiscal Times report wrote that casino revenue from Atlantic City has been roughly halved since 2007. Keith Foley, a Moody's Investor Service Casino Analyst said that the drop in Atlantic City casino revenue was something on one saw coming. The June 8 2014 article from The Fiscal Times reported that the American Gaming Association said that the total U.S. casino revenue in 2012 was less than a ten year peak set in 2007.

Imagine the revenue casinos bring in if there are more of them in the market.   On July 1st 2014, the New York Times reported that 17 applications were received by the New York State Gaming Commission.   In 2013 a law passed accepting casino gambling in the state. Four of the applications came from Mohegan Sun, Hard Rock International, Penn National Gaming and Caesars Entertainment.   The report also indicates that although casinos are being developed for Massachusetts and New York, casino revenues have been found on a sliding decline in neighboring New Jersey and Connecticut.

With casino revenue declining in existing venues, does it make sense to add more with the known risks of crime increase from theft caused by addicted gamblers?   Will the cost to the tax payer be worth it? Declining revenue means low paying casino jobs with eventual layoffs. Unemployment insurance covers a portion of the low paying job.   A near poverty income that is lost will put families into poverty. Are the long term risks worth it?

Layoffs and Lost Job Opportunities

Casinos that are new to an area make promises of job creation.   As with the law of supply and demand, initially there is the appearance of an abundance of jobs and so the pay is very low or at minimum wage. However, just like any other business there are layoffs. With competing casinos in Connecticut, the jobs in Western, Massachusetts are expected to be few in number and low in pay.   In addition there are layoffs expected in the long term.

In the first quarter of 2013, Foxwoods reported through WFSB-TV (Eyewitness News 3) that they would be laying off workers due to what they say is due to as the CEO Scott Butera said "increased competition and a presently declining market."   He went on to say ""We are focused on efficiency of operations at all levels in order to achieve success in today's challenging environment and to sustain that success well into the future with a goal of supporting strong employment levels for years to come,".

About a year later, Foxwoods reported through the Associated Press on May 15, 2014 that they would be cutting hours and have possible layoffs.   A memo to employees obtained by the associated press indicated that there would be "staffing changes across all levels of employment."   This change was also reported on the same day by WTNH News 8 in Connecticut.   Earlier reports show that layoffs happened before at Foxwoods for example the Associated Press reported that layoffs would affect approximately 2% of the 10,000 employees. The workers were laid off on June 26 of that year.   The job cuts occurred a month after Foxwoods opened its new MGM Grand Casino. In this same report by the Associated Press, Mohegan Sun had reduced its workforce by a few hundred through attrition.   At the time of this report, Analyst Dennis Forst of Key Banc Capital Markets said that Las Vegas customers had begun to cut back due to economic concerns.   He also reported that all US gaming markets spending was down and expected the trend to continue.

In the fourth quarter of 2012, Mohegan Sun announced layoffs on NBC Connecticut and Cape Cod Times.   The layoffs were reported to be 328 by the end of October

2012 (George Brennan of Cape Cod Times). Two years earlier, the casino laid off 350 workers. In 2012, the Massachusetts Gaming Commission Chairman Stephen Crosby had declined an interview about the Mohegan Sun Layoffs.

NBC channel 10 in Philadelphia announced on Friday, June 27 that Showboat Hotel and Casino in Atlantic City plans to close leaving 2,000 employees unemployed. Philly.com reported on June 21, 2014 that Revel Casino Hotel in Atlantic City had been operating at a loss since their opening in 2012 and had filed for its second bankruptcy. The New York Times reported on May 31, 2014, Harrah's Tunica casino in Tunica Resorts, Mississippi was scheduled to close affecting up to 950 employees. The report analyzed that there are too many casinos chasing too few gambling dollars. This New York Times article interviewed a 66 year old man who worked at the casino for 18 years who said "I don't have anywhere else to go. Nobody's going to hire me."

.

Gambling Addiction and Crime

A gambling addiction is called Ludomania which is an urge to continue gambling despite the negative consequences.   Dr. Roxanne Dryden-Edwards and Dr. William C Shiel Jr. reports on onhealth.com that compulsive gambling affects 2% to 5% of Americans. The affected individuals find that they need continuously more money for gambling to satisfy the gambling enjoyment.   The enjoyment comes from escaping problems ore relieving sadness or anxiety.   When money is lost, the individual works harder at gambling to recoup the loss. It is an ongoing cycle. To finance the gambling, the individual reverts to crime through stealing, fraud, or forgery to acquire finances. This high focused attention on gambling results in lost marriages and employment.

Did you know that casinos inherently have crime associated with them?   Casinos thrive on money being wagered and an addicted gambler will need a lot of it. Once they run out of their own, they will do whatever it takes to get more. Theft is the answer in the case of desperation. The behavior is almost like the addiction to drugs. Instead of drugs, the fuel for the addiction for gambling is money.

In Canada, the Edmonton Journal reported on June 27, 2014 that a man stole more than $126,000 from his employer, Raynor Rentals, to support his gambling addiction. The man worked at the company as an accountant. In 2011, he began gambling and a year later the addiction was out of control. He was sentences to jail for six months followed by two years of probation. He is also sentenced to counselling and 75 hours of community service. Family members had paid the $126,000 to the employer.

Here is a partial repeat of an earlier chapter to give perspective:

On February 26, 2012, The Associated Press reported on crime rates around Connecticut casinos since openings. In 1992, Foxwoods opened and in 1996 Mohegan Sun opened. In 2011 Mohegan Sun generated $719 million in slot machine revenue and Foxwoods generated $650 million in slot machine revenue. Prior to the opening, Governor Lowell Weicker warned in 1991 that the opening of Foxwoods in 1992 would lead to crime, prostitution, drunk driving, and other related crime. After Foxwoods, the first casino opened, thefts rose substantially with larcenies accounting for most of the crimes. Today, Larceny is the largest theft crime among both casinos. Embezzlements have more than tripled due most likely to gambling debts. Connecticut averages about 158 embezzlement annually. Before the casinos, the number of reported embezzlements cases averaged around 49.

Gambling Illness

On March 25, 2013 the Republican Newspaper (Springfield, MA) reported Massachusetts has axed $560,000 from that fiscal year's budget for the Massachusetts Council on Compulsive Gambling, the state's main prevention and treatment program.

Dot Duda, the director of Outpatient Psychiatry and the Prevention and Recovery Center at Mount Auburn Hospital in Cambridge said in the same newspaper report "We have ha people who are suicidal". She goes on to say, "We have no place to send them".

The article on March 25, 2013 from the Republican (Springfield, MA) has also reported that the Massachusetts Council of Compulsive Gambling estimates that between 85,000 to 185,000 residents of the state have at least one time in their lives experienced disorderly gambling.   A national organization called The National Gambling Impact Study Commission estimates the number of addicted or problem gamblers doubles within 50 miles of a new casino or slot complex.   A 2004 study by the University of Buffalo's Research Institute of Additions found that the rates double again within 10 miles of a casino.   The Republican newspaper (same article) report that these two findings are routinely used by experts to evaluate casinos impact to a community.

The Desert Effect

For the moment, let's discuss how Springfield, Massachusetts would be affected by MGM creating a large casino in downtown Springfield. Picture for a moment, a casino towering in Springfield and how that may impact the surrounding towns and cities within the Pioneer Valley. Think of how far south, including Enfield, Connecticut, the impact can be felt.

The effect of casino gaming can be stretched quite a distance. Many cars in Connecticut's Foxwoods and Mohegan Sun have Massachusetts, Rhode Island, and New York license plates. There is a daily high volume of out of state traffic. Now think of the license plates that will be seen at a Springfield, Massachusetts casino. The interstate I-90 brings in traffic from the Hudson Valley and Albany, New York region. Coming from the North, travelers from Southern Vermont will make an easy trek down interstate I-91. The single purpose of casino gaming will increase out of state traffic on interstates to crowd the city of Springfield. Those with gambling addictions don't worry how far they have to travel. Traffic from New Hampshire and Rhode Island will increase traffic to the already busy Boston area if Casinos are placed on the Eastern part of the state.

When many people think of casinos, they think of the Las Vegas strip in the desert.   When I think of Casinos coming into town, I think of the same reaction that small businesses and communities react when a Walmart or Home Depot comes into town. It usually isn't favorable in small towns.   There are news reports across the country showing the resistance due to impact to small businesses and traffic congestion.   Those news reports include the controversy of Walmart's plan to build a superstore in Holyoke, Massachusetts.   The residents don't want a change to a more central location that drives people to the big shopping centers like a Walmart or Home Depot.

Let's for a moment look at a former proposed plan for Walmart to build a supercenter in Holyoke, Massachusetts.   This will illustrate how big business effects a small city. A MassLive.com report on August 4, 2013 talked about the concern of exploited workers and small businesses being steamrolled with Walmart's low prices.   The report wrote that the organization Stop Walmart in Holyoke claimed "low-waged workers must get government subsidies to survive and Walmart's low prices hurt the economy by driving out existing businesses."   In July 2013 about 100 neighbors, labor union members, and politicians attended a protest to fight against Walmart's plan to open a supercenter on Whiting Farms Road.   The concern was that a 160,000 square foot Walmart would increase traffic congestion around the Holyoke Mall at Ingleside.   The holiday traffic was of biggest concern.   Holyoke Mayor Alex B. Morse initially welcomed the idea of Walmart, but weeks later sided with the anti-Walmart movement.   The Masslive.com report quoted the Mayor of Holyoke as saying, "The net benefit of Walmart is nonexistent ..." By September of 2013, Walmart retreated from their proposed supercenter in Holyoke.   The proposed Big Y store that had been considered on schedule earlier in 2012 was cancelled also in September of 2013.   Now imagine the Holyoke situation in Springfield and instead of a Walmart, it is MGM and casino gaming.   The concerns Holyoke, Massachusetts had is only magnified in the larger city of Springfield, Massachusetts.   Have we learned anything from Holyoke and can we apply it to Springfield.   Or have we forgotten and run the risk of ruin if we allow MGM to come to Springfield, Massachusetts.

Now think of the size of Foxwoods and Mohegan Suns in Connecticut. Imagine that in Springfield. Does it seem the impact would be worse? Can you imagine families wanting to have a casino down the street from their schools? If they leave then residential life in Springfield will dry up. The families that stay behind, what do you think will happen to them?

Let's think of how Springfield's casino would impact the local Springfield neighborhood community. Do you really think families will want their children going to schools so close to a casino? With high theft caused by addicted gamblers, the crime rate would be significantly higher. Is the environment of a casino a place where we want our children to grow up? Will families want to be in an area of high traffic congestion? There would be fewer alternatives for shopping as small businesses would be pushed out due to costs or traffic. Eventually many families would migrate out of the area and this would change the demographic of the area. Inner

Springfield will only be suitable for the function of casino gaming.

A MassLive.com report on July 2, 2014 reported that a Western Massachusetts casino would hurt home values. The Realtor Association of Pioneer Value reported that a home in a casino community would cost homeowners from $1,650 to $3,300 in lost value. This study was prepared by economists at the National Association of Realtors.

Business Staff Resources Lost to Casinos

Let's accept for the moment that the MGM casino provides a flourishing buffet of jobs in Springfield, Massachusetts. The labor is pulled in from the local area reducing the unemployment in that area. Many jobs that a casino would offer require skills that other companies would benefit from. However, if the unemployment is reduced significantly, by the proposed thousands of jobs created, then the pool of available qualified talent is reduced for other area businesses in surrounding towns. Eventually, some of those businesses would not be able to operate with the staffing available. Some businesses would close.

If a business closes, then there is less opportunity in the event someone loses a job at a casino due to future attrition, layoff, or other matter. Their chances of finding a job is less likely now as the only major employer is MGM.

Many of the skilled labor comes from outside of the area and does not benefit the local residents who may not be fitted or qualified for a job at MGM. The unemployment rate is the number of unemployed divided by the workforce. If the number of unemployed locally remains the same, but the size of the workforce is increased from out-of-towners, then the measured unemployment rate would be less. The number of locally unemployed stays the same, but unemployment rate goes down because of workers who travel from Vermont, New York, Connecticut who will work at MGM in Springfield.

This lower unemployment rate gives a false sense of security for those locally unemployed individuals. This rate does not measure the local unemployment rate. It is measurement of the geographic rather than the demographic, i.e. those who live locally.

The Mayor of Springfield may say that the unemployment in Springfield will go down. He is less likely to say that the number of people unemployed in Springfield will go down. He will say that the opportunities for jobs are available. He is less likely able to have MGM higher only within Springfield only.

It is MGM that determines where it will get its workforce. They may be obligated to interview Springfield residents first, but at the end of the day, the final choice is up to MGM for talent no matter where they come from.

Depending on talent needed, MGM's arrival to Springfield could in fact deplete employment opportunities for a certain demographic in the region. Over time if someone left Foxwoods or Mohegan Sun in Connecticut, they would be trained and qualified to work at MGM in Springfield, Massachusetts and vice versa.

Not only will local area businesses lose a pool of talent to hire, they would also lose customers.   There is only so much consumer money to go around.   Whatever goes to the casino would be lost in area businesses.

A business that loses employee talent and consumers would not be able to be sustained for an extended period of time.   Eventually, the dynamics of lack of staffing that is unmatched with a reduced cliental would hurt the business.

Local Government Budgets

Your local government would like you to believe that money that is earmarked for a good cause like education would increase revenue for education. Money that is earmarked for a program doesn't necessarily increase revenue for that program.

Here is an example. Let's pretend there are parents who have a child in college who spends $10 per week on pizza. The parents send $5 a week to support pizza with the intention that the child will now have $15 per week on pizza. The child uses the $5 from the parents for pizza while at the same time takes $5 from their existing $10 budget for pizza and moves it to cigarette purchases. So the additional $5 from the parents is used for pizza, but $5 from the original $10 was subtracted and move it to a bad habit, ie something not good. The end result is the pizza budget remains the same at $10 per week and now $5 is being used on something wasteful.

The pizza example happens in government too. An amount of money may be earmarked for education for example.   That dollar amount would shift away from the current budget to something else leaving the education budget unchanged.   For example, if revenue from MGM includes $50,000 earmarked for education, then the budget for education would be reduced by $50,000 to satisfy other budget needs. The end result is the budget for education is unchanged.   Does the public see this?   Of course not.   We vote people into office, but don't tell them how to do their job when they get there.

On May 19, 2014, MassLive.com reported that $581.9 million budget for the 2015 fiscal year that had no layoffs, maintains essential services, and funds the vacancies for police and firefighter funds.   The article also reports that the budget was balanced using $2.8 million reserve funds. MassLive.com also reported that in the past 3 years, Springfield used a total of $23.6 mi from the stabilization fund to help balance those budgets.   That stabilization or reserve funds is where that extra "pizza" money goes to allow for shifting of funds.   Earmarked funds does not necessarily mean increased funds for a particular program or department.

A Crowded Casino Market

Years ago, Western Massachusetts experienced casino gambling in one place.   People travel to Foxwoods and Mohegan Suns to satisfy their gambling entertainment fix.   Mohegan Sun and Foxwoods Resort are 11 miles apart along Route 2.   The travel time between the two casinos is less than 20 minutes.   The distance between the Massachusetts/Connecticut border at I-91 to the Casinos is over 72 miles and takes about an hour and a half to get there by car.   If you go to Foxwoods or Mohegan Sun, you will see a lot of cars with Massachusetts license plates.   That means there are people who travel more than 70 miles for more than an hour and a half to get there.   Imagine the traffic flow to Springfield, Massachusetts if MGM were to be built. Start from Springfield and go out 70 plus miles or a 90 minute drive.   That traffic would be coming to Springfield.   How do you think that would impact local schools? What do you think your daily local commute on the road would be like?

The   Western,   Massachusetts   casino   gaming environment would be saturated.   Already there are two casinos in Connecticut about 90 minute from Springfield, Massachusetts. Fox Business News reported on July 1, 2014 that the review of 17 applications for 4 casinos in New York will begin. The 4 New York casinos are proposed to be divided among three regions: the Albany-Saratoga area, the Southern Tier-Finger Lakes region and the Catskills and mid-Hudson River Valley.

With Casino revenues slipping in Connecticut and New Jersey, how will casinos in Western, Massachusetts and New York be successful? Does it make sense that this crowded market can impact the future of casino success? Already, casinos are slowly beginning to close affecting a significantly large number of people.

Here is a partial repeat of an earlier chapter to give perspective:

In the fourth quarter of 2012, Mohegan Sun announced layoffs on NBC Connecticut and Cape Cod Times. The layoffs were reported to be 328 by the end of October 2012 (George Brennan of Cape Cod Times). Two years earlier, the casino laid off 350 workers. In 2012, the Massachusetts Gaming Commission Chairman Stephen

Crosby had declined an interview about the Mohegan Sun Layoffs.

NBC channel 10 in Philadelphia announced on Friday, June 27 that Showboat Hotel and Casino in Atlantic City plans to close leaving 2,000 employees unemployed. Philly.com reported on June 21, 2014 that Revel Casino Hotel in Atlantic City had been operating at a loss since their opening in 2012 and had filed for its second bankruptcy. The New York Times reported on May 31, 2014, Harrah's Tunica casino in Tunica Resorts, Mississippi was scheduled to close affecting up to 950 employees.   The report analyzed that there are too many casinos chasing too few gambling dollars.   This New York Times article interviewed a 66 year old man who worked at the casino for 18 years who said "I don't have anywhere else to go. Nobody's going to hire me."

Do You Need More?

The contents of this book have enough of a starting point to formulate an understanding of the dangers of having a casino in a small city like Springfield, Massachusetts. What is contained here are facts that have already been reported in the news that are easily verifiable. A much larger book isn't needed to formulate an educated understanding of the impact of casino gaming within our community.

Learn more beyond this book by doing your own search on news using Google:

http://news.google.com (News Google Search Engine)

To write this book, I spent time looking at the facts by looking at the reported news. Let this book serve as a stepping stone to your own research and education.

Follow our progress at:

ProjectFurious2014.BlogSpot.com

Project Furious 2014

With the understanding that actions speak louder than words, PROJECT FURIOUS 2014 has adopted the slogan "Share if You Care"

ProjectFurious2014.BlogSpot.com

www.Facebook.com/ProjectFurious2014

www.ingramcontent.com/pod-product-compliance
Lightning Source LLC
Chambersburg PA
CBHW071647170526
45166CB00003B/1470